DOG SCOUTS OF AMERICA

by Shelley Bueche and Chris Puls

BEARPORT
PUBLISHING

New York, New York

Credits

Cover and Title Page, © Tom Uhlman Photography; Cover (RT), © Mandy Hall; Cover (RM), © Chris Puls; Cover (RB), © Joanne Weber; Table of Contents, © Joanne Weber; 4, © Tom Uhlman Photography; 5, © Tom Uhlman Photography; 6, © Tom Uhlman Photography; 7, © Mike Puls; 8, © Joanne Weber; 9, © Photo by Joanne Weber, card courtesy of Chris Puls; 10, © Mandy Hall; 11, © Mandy Hall; 12, © Cindy Ratliff; 13, © Joanne Weber; 14A, © Mandy Hall; 14B, © Tom Uhlman Photography; 15, © Cindy Ratliff; 16, © Mandy Hall; 17, © Joanne Weber; 18, © Joanne Weber; 19, © Nancy Strack; 20, © Courtesy of The PawZone, Liberty, Missouri; 21, ©; Mandy Hall 22, © Mandy Hall; 23, © Mandy Hall; 24, © Irving (TX) Fire Department, courtesy of Cindy Ratliff; 25, © Joanne Weber; 26, © Grace Stevens; 27, © Gerry Duffy; 29A, © Robert Pearcy/Animals Animals-Earth Scenes; 29B, © Photodisc/Fotosearch.com; 29C, © Photospin.com; 29D, © Fotosearch.com; 29E, © Tim Davis/Photo Researchers, Inc.; 29F, © Jorg & Petra Wegner/Animals Animals-Earth Scenes; 31, © Dog Scouts of America.

Publisher: Kenn Goin
Senior Editor: Lisa Wiseman
Creative Director: Spencer Brinker
Photo Researcher: Amy Dunleavy
Original Design: Dawn Beard Creative

Library of Congress Cataloging-in-Publication Data

Bueche, Shelley.
 Dog Scouts of America / by Shelley Bueche and Chris Puls.
   p. cm. — (Dog heroes)
 Includes bibliographical references and index.
 ISBN-13: 978-1-59716-625-6 (library binding)
 ISBN-10: 1-59716-625-1 (library binding)
 1. Dog Scouts of America. 2. Service dogs—United States. 3. Service dogs—Training.
 I. Puls, Chris. II. Title.

 HV1569.6.B84 2008
 636.7'0835—dc22

                          2007041793

For more information, write to Bearport Publishing Company, Inc., 101 Fifth Avenue, Suite 6R, New York, New York 10003. Printed in the United States of America.

10 9 8 7 6 5 4 3 2 1

Table of Contents

Bear

It was a cold fall day. A small beagle was wandering alone on a road in Indiana. He was wet and hungry. He was looking for **shelter** from the icy cold rain.

Bear in Indiana

The dog had not had an easy life. He had never lived in a house before. He had never had **training** or love from a person. However, this dog's luck was about to change.

This beagle was named Baron von Beaglestein, or Bear for short.

A New Home

Soon, Bear saw a truck on the road and ran up to it. Mike Puls was inside. He took one look at the cold, wet dog and brought him home. Mike and his family soon **adopted** Bear.

Chris Puls giving Bear the hand signal for "sit"

Bear was loved and cared for by his new family. However, he had to learn important skills in order to live with people. Bear didn't even know how to walk down stairs!

Mike's wife, Chris, taught Bear how to understand hand and word signals. Chris used these **cues** to tell Bear to sit, lie down, stay, **heel**, and come. The cues helped Bear become a well-behaved dog.

Dogs are very smart. Some scientists believe that they are nearly as smart as two-year-old children.

Chris Puls teaching Bear to "heel"

The Test

Chris knew how to train dogs because of the work she had done with Dog Scouts of America (DSA). This group helps owners such as Chris teach their dogs good behavior. When an owner feels a dog is ready, the animal can take the special DSA test. It measures whether the dog can follow cues such as "lie down" or "stay." The test also makes sure that the owner can care for and control the animal.

During one part of the DSA test, dogs have to walk past other animals and not bother them.

Bear took the Dog Scout test over three meetings. It was hard, but Bear passed. He was now an **official** Dog Scout.

"Let us learn new things that we may be more helpful."
Dog Scout Motto

This card issued June 25, 2005 certifies:

Bear

has passed a test for exemplary behavior conducted by

Dog Scouts of America

and is thereby given the title of

Dog Scout

www.dogscouts.org

Dog Scouts of America reserves the right to revoke certification at its discretion.

Bear's official Dog Scouts of America card

When an owner joins the DSA and agrees to properly care for and train his dog, then the pet becomes a Cadet Scout.

The Beginning

Bear and Chris became one of many dog-and-owner teams that are part of the DSA. This group has many important goals. One goal is to teach dog owners how to train and care for their animals. Another goal is to give dogs and owners a chance to help their **communities**.

Lisa and her dog Buttercup, a DSA team, prepare to go on a hike.

A group of Dog Scouts and owners from the same area form a **troop**. Today, there are more than 60 DSA troops in the United States, Canada, and Japan.

Lonnie Olson came up with the idea of starting a group for dogs and their owners in 1995. She enjoyed swimming, hiking, and boating with her dog Karli. She wanted to meet other people who liked doing the same things with their pets. So she **founded** the Dog Scouts of America.

Lonnie Olson and her new puppy, Kozi

True Troopers

Anyone can join a Dog Scout troop with his or her dog. The dog's owner pays a small **fee** to become a member. However, a dog cannot become a Dog Scout until he or she passes the DSA test. Some dog-and-owner teams already have many skills when they join. These dogs usually pass the test right away. Others have fewer skills and must train before taking the test.

Dog Scouts and their owners on a 6-mile (10-km) hike

Troop life is a very important part of the DSA. Some troops go on hikes or campouts. Others go swimming, kayaking, or play games. Many hold **fund-raisers** to earn money for other animals in need. There is one thing all troops have in common, though. All Dog Scout troops work together to learn skills and have fun.

Beth and her Dog Scout Reggie on a kayak

Willie Weber was a Dog Scout with Troop 101 in Michigan. This golden retriever was famous in his community for raising money. He appeared on television and even had his own fan club.

Earning Badges

Once a dog becomes a Dog Scout, he or she begins to work on earning **badges**. A DSA badge is a small round piece of cloth that can be sewn onto the dog's scarf or vest. The badge shows that the dog has learned a new skill.

DSA badges

Casie works with Libby on her swimming.

14

Some badges are awarded for fun activities such as hiking, swimming, or even painting. Other badges are earned for learning more serious skills. For example, a manners badge proves that a Dog Scout has learned not to jump on people. It shows that the dog will lie on a mat when told. A first aid badge proves that an owner knows how to care for his or her dog. It also shows that the dog will accept care if he is hurt.

Mandy watches Simon paint.

Dog Scouts can earn a badge called "The Art of Shaping." Dogs use a sponge attached to a bootie that is dipped in paint to create art.

Dog Sports

Dog Scouts love to get a lot of exercise! Dog Scout owners believe that when a dog is tired from playing and learning, he or she is less likely to get into trouble.

A Dog Scout making his way through an obstacle course

This is why sports are important to the Dog Scouts. Dogs learn **agility** by climbing through **obstacle courses**. They build up their speed and strength by pulling sleds. They even play Frisbee by catching the flying disks in the air. All Dog Scouts have a chance to try these exciting activities.

DSA dogs enjoy going sledding during winter camp.

Some sports are best for small dogs. Others are better for large dogs. However, a dog can try any sport through the DSA. If a tiny dog shows interest in helping to pull a sled, he or she learns how to do so safely.

Dogs Help Out

Dog Scouts do more than just play and learn new skills. Dog Scout teams also help people in their towns or cities. DSA teams may raise money for good causes. For example, a dog-and-owner team may gather **donations** for a group that is helping to fight **cancer**. When a person offers money to a Dog Scout, the animal gently takes the money in his or her mouth. Then the dog puts the money into a bucket. Some Dog Scouts do tricks to earn donations!

Willie Weber, from Troop 101, rings a bell to help collect donations for the Salvation Army.

NOW OPEN

HOURS

Dog Scouts may also visit people in hospitals. Simon is a 120-pound (54-kg) Great Dane from Texas. He and his owner, Mandy, visit **patients** at a children's hospital. Children who are ill are happy to get a visit from a friendly dog like Simon.

Dogs like Daisy (left) and Gus (right), from Troop 119 in Texas, help bring cheer to people in hospitals and nursing homes.

Troop 121 in Miami, Florida, helps out by working with Girl Scouts. The Girl Scouts and Dog Scouts visit a local pet supply store. There, they show customers how to train their own dogs at home.

Reading with Dogs

Dog Scouts have even helped kids learn to read! The DSA has a reading program called SIRIUS. These letters stand for Scouts Improve Reading Interest, Understanding, and Skills. In this program, dogs and their owners go to libraries to help children read.

Hero, a Dog Scout, reads with Amber and Candace at school.

Kids read short books to the Dog Scouts at the library. The dogs listen quietly, which helps young readers relax. A child may be less nervous reading to a dog than to a parent or teacher. Kids enjoy getting to know the dogs, too. Having a dog to read to makes some children want to read more.

Courtney reads with Simon at the Flower Mound Public Library in Texas.

Dogs trained to help people feel better are often called therapy dogs.

Camp for Dogs

A trip to DSA camp can be a great reward for a dog. Any member of the DSA can bring his or her dog to camp. The camps are always small, with about 40 dog-and-owner teams. Summer camps may last a whole week. Shorter camps are held in the fall.

Schwartz (left) and Simon (right) have fun at camp.

While at camp, dogs get to stay with their owners. The team eats together, learns new skills, works on earning badges, and spends evenings by a campfire. They also have a chance to make friends with other Dog Scout teams. Everyone has a great time at camp.

Julie and her dog, Pico, training at camp

As the DSA grows, more camps are being planned around the world. The most popular camps, called mini-camps, take place over weekends.

23

Some Special Troops

Troop 119 from Texas is the largest DSA troop in the world, with more than 100 dogs and owners. It raises money to buy special oxygen masks for the Dallas Fire Department. The masks help pets that are **injured** in fires breathe better.

Cindy and her dog, BJ, show how the special oxygen masks work.

Troop 107 from Ohio raises money to buy bulletproof vests for police dogs. They have raised as much as $550 in just four hours. They get the money by receiving donations from people who want to help. At some fund-raisers, each dog has his or her own bucket. The dogs are trained to put money only in their own buckets. Coyote, an eight-year-old cattle dog, has raised more than $9,000! He gets a small treat for each donation.

Angel, a Dog Scout from Illinois, is helping raise funds for a DSA educational program.

On August 24, 2006, a tiny four-pound (2-kg) Chihuahua almost died in a fire. Smoke got in his lungs. The fire department helped him breathe with a small oxygen mask from Troop 119. His life was saved!

Looking Ahead

Many DSA members say that kids are the future dog trainers of the world. Kids aged 6 to 18 can even become Junior Scouts.

Junior Scouts work with their pets to take the Dog Scout test. The test changes depending on the age of the child. For example, a seven-year-old Junior Scout may give a dog a treat as a reward for lying down. However, a 14-year-old child should be able to get the dog to lie down without a treat. The rules are different because young children cannot always control dogs as easily as older children and adults.

Richelle and Oreo were the first Junior Scout team.

As the DSA becomes more popular, more troops are planned. Teams join every year to support the goals of the DSA. By learning to love and respect one another, all Dog Scouts and owners gain benefits for a lifetime.

Troop 107

Some Dog Scouts are huge! Halo and BleuSkye, Rottweilers from Troop 135 in Missouri, each weigh more than 100 pounds (45 kg).

Just the Facts

- Karli, a Border collie owned by Lonnie Olson, was the first dog to earn a Dog Scout badge.

- Troop 119 from Texas visits schools to talk about pet care. They show kids how to stay safe around dogs, too. For example, they allow children to practice walking up to a Dog Scout's owner and asking if it is okay to pet the animal. This helps children avoid getting bitten.

- Chelsea and her owner, Kat, belong to Troop 130 in Michigan. They have earned a badge in sign language. When Kat puts her palms together next to her tilted head, Chelsea knows it's time to go to sleep.

- Many troops care for homeless pets. Troop 143 in Austin, Texas, found a homeless dog named Sweetie. The troop cared for Sweetie and her puppies until they were adopted.

- Some Dog Scouts like to perform tricks. Maverick, a papillon, and Happy, a Jack Russell terrier, are from Troop 104 in Michigan. They work with their owner to perform funny skits at camp. In one skit, the dogs pretend to be part of a three-ring circus!

Common Breeds: DOG SCOUTS

Australian shepherd

German shepherd

golden retriever

Labrador retriever

beagle

Border collie

Glossary

adopted (uh-DOPT-id) taken into one's family

agility (uh-JILL-uh-tee) the ability to move quickly and easily

badges (BAJ-iz) small round pieces of cloth that can be sewn onto a dog's scarf or vest

cancer (KAN-sur) a disease that happens when a person's body makes cells that are not normal

communities (kuh-MYOO-nuh-teez) a group of people living in the same area

cues (KYOOZ) signals used to explain something

donations (doh-NAY-shuhnz) money that is given to help a good cause

fee (FEE) the amount of money someone is charged for a service

founded (FOUND-id) started something, such as a group or school

fund-raisers (FUHND-rayz-urz) events that raise money for good causes

heel (HEEL) when a dog walks on the left side of a person

injured (IN-jurd) hurt

obstacle courses (OB-stuh-kuhl KORSS-iz) training courses filled with hurdles, fences, and walls that dogs must get through

official (uh-FISH-uhl) approved by the people who are in charge

patients (PAY-shuhnts) people who are receiving medical care from a doctor

shelter (SHEL-tur) a place where a person or animal is protected

training (TRANE-ing) the teaching of new skills

troop (TROOP) a group of people or animals

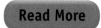
Bibliography

Mann, Susan E. *Kippy: Second Chance Dog.* West Conshohocken, PA: Infinity Publishing.com (2005).

Weston, Ruth, and Dr. Catriona Ross. *Kids & Dogs.* Melbourne, Victoria, Australia: Allen & Unwin (2004).

Read More

American Kennel Club. *The Complete Dog Book for Kids.* New York: Hungry Minds, Inc. (1996).

Tagliaferro, Linda. *Service Dogs (Dog Heroes).* New York: Bearport Publishing (2005).

Tagliaferro, Linda. *Therapy Dogs (Dog Heroes).* New York: Bearport Publishing (2005).

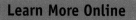
Learn More Online

Visit this Web site to learn more about Dog Scouts:
www.dogscouts.org

Index

About the Authors

Shelley Bueche is a children's book author who enjoys writing about dogs. She and her family share their home with three canine companions, Belle, Brownie, and Boomer, in Austin, Texas. Shelley has attended Dog Scout meetings in her hometown and is interested in joining the Dog Scouts of America in the future.

Chris Puls has been training dogs for more than 25 years and currently has five of her own. She discovered Dog Scouts of America in 2000 and started a troop in 2001. Chris will become the president of the DSA in 2008. She loves to help people and dogs learn new things.